Sensuous Poems Through Time

by

Renne' Fletcher Siewers

Sensuous Poems Through Time tells the story of life's loves, hardships, emotions, and passions. Each poem tells a story of a person or event in the cross roads of life. The written words are an outlet for pain, happiness, and confusion. Interpret these messages into your life for comfort throughout time.

Dedicated to all the people who have traversed the many pathways of life events; *Love Today*, *Going Away*, and *Life Disarray*.

I want to thank my wonderful husband, Jon Siewers, for supporting me unconditionally throughout our journey together.

2012 by Renne' Fletcher Siewers
All rights reserved. No part of this book may be reproduced, stored in a retrieval system, or transmitted in any form or by any means without the prior written permission of the author.

ISBN-13: 978-1480070004

ISBN-10: 1480070009

Sensuous Poems Through Time *by Renne'*

TABLE OF CONTENTS

LOVING TODAY   6

The Rain   7

Raining in my Soul   8

Dancing   9

Yesterday's Encounter   10

Winding Love   11

Field of Life   16

The Confident Man   17

Missing You   23

My Valentine   25

The Mystery   28

Love   32

Secrets   33

Valentine   35

GOING AWAY   36

River of Friends   37

The Eclipse   38

Howling at the Moon   40

The Beach   44

Waves   45

Time	46
Tijuana	47
Clear Blue Water	48
Wispy Clouds	51
Hidden Away	53
Caribbean Music	55
Take Me Caribbean	56
Seeking	58
Paradise	59
Belize	61
The Ride	62
Harvest Moon Delight	63
Chihuahua	65
LIFE DISARRAY	**67**
Looking Out the Window	68
Naked	69
The Fear	71
A Little Girl	72
Say Good-bye to Silence	73
My Son	74
Take Me Wind	76
Shadows	77

Sensuous Poems Through Time *by Renne'*

Change O' Heart	78
Rejoice	79
The Sadness	80
Wispy Clouds	82
Messages	84
A Silent Kiss	85
Words	87
Silence	88
Stand Still My Husband	90
The Mask	91
Can You Hear?	93
Life	94
PASSING TO STAY	**95**
Large Foreheads	96
Thirty Years	97
Delicate Rose	98
Flying High	99
The Artist Within	100
Images	101
The Collector	102
Guiding Light	103

Loving Today

The Rain

Wetness surrounding her body
One drop falling at a time
Endless thoughts roll to the sea
Seeking softly words that rhyme
One drop falling at a time

Feel the warmth touching
Feel the warmth brushing

Across the fingers to her lips
Rolling toward sensuous hips

Shimmering droplets from within
Glimmering droplets from within

Of wetness surrounding her body
One drop falling at a time
Endless thoughts roll to the sea
Hearing lightly words that rhyme
One drop falling at a time

Feel the cool singing
Feel the cool bringing

Engulfed throughout your life
Seeking solitude while in strife

Shimmering droplets from within
Glimmering droplets from within

(continued)

Of wetness surrounding her body
One drop falling at a time
Endless thoughts rolled to sea
Breaking through the words that rhyme
One drop falling at a time

Feel the heat chasing
Feel the heat raising

Wetness in a kiss hovering
From head to toe covering

Shimmering droplets from within
Glimmering droplets from within

Of wetness surrounding her body
One drop falling at a time
Endless thoughts crush to the sea
Screaming out words that rhyme
One drop falling at a time

Feel the love lying
Feel the love hiding

The last drop fell upon her head
Seeking solace within his bed

Shimmering droplets from within
Glimmering droplets from within

Raining in my Soul

Dancing

The bright lights dance across the sky
Twinkling, glimmering in my eyes
Softly moving with the motion
Contemplating the blue ocean

This place tucked away in the desert
Away from home disguising the warm heart
Drinking of the deep red wine
Missing laughter lost in time

The soft lights dance across the sky
Twinkling, glimmering in my eyes
Wishing my sweet love was here
Sitting next to me to share

My heart so lonely tonight
Waiting until morning light
When I will come back home to you
Into your arms, faithful and true

The dim lights dance across the sky
Twinkling, glimmering in my eyes
Only to feel your warm sensuous kiss
Naked tenderly returning to bliss

Dancing in the Light

Yesterday's Encounter

Encounter the past
Meet the future
Happiness at last

Glowing, touching, reaching
Within sunshine teaching
Take both my hands
Time slipping sands

Encounter today
Meet tomorrow
Happiness I pray

Sharing seeking playing
As if to be making
Laugher to the wind
Hearts that shall blend

Encounter yesterday
Meet infinity
Happiness always stays

Smiling seeking laughing
Giggling whispering
With moments of time
Stolen to be mine

Today's Encounter

Sensuous Poems Through Time *by Renne'*

Winding Love

Winding Love of two
Which one should I choose?
Both in the mid-life prime
Waiting for a certain sign

Gasping Love of two
Both wanting I do
One a love that was lost
The other sent not to boss

Twisted Love of two
Intertwined through and through
How should I handle each?
Both distance not to reach

Fanning Love of two
Each I want so true
Seeking security to share
Throughout the years to care

Breathless Love of two
Make me sure of you
Take my hand and guide the way
Take me safe though the day

Twisted Love of two
Pick one, which will do
Both handsome, devoted too
But neither can for you

(continued)

Whisking Love of two
Tell both adieus
And live silently along
Telling neither they are gone

Thus losing Love of two
Shall always make me blue
Choose I must and choose I will
Keeping fantasy real

Winding Love

Friends

Friends met, loved and parted
To embrace without fear
To speak unspoken words
About life, challenges and dreams
To seek nothing more than friendship

Friends to care with feelings
Of happiness and safety
Allowing thoughts beyond boundaries
Of commitment, just to be friends
In the world of Fantasy
I reach out my hand
For you to take
My fellow friend

Forever Friends

Forgotten Way

I shed a tear
Far long ago
When left with fear
Each drops that flow

Through the blindness
Of love cherished
Memories that won't fade
Try, try as I made
Each day into night
No hope without light
May tomorrow be today?
And today tomorrow
In happiness and play
No more tainted with sorrow

Trust in love, the hope, the person
Brightness, daylight, sunshine
All together and one
Forever will thee be mine

With the Forgotten Way

Safe Inside

The touch that links us together

Answers not questions

Making what was now forever

Wholeness in sanction

Reach for my hand always knowing

Sanction in Believing

In the look, the smile, the loving

Believing the searching

Every inch covered in kisses

Searching the ending

Beginning with the ecstasy

Safe inside resounding

Safe Inside

Field of Life

Walk along the crooked path
Blue bells growing neatly
Singly one or two in math
Rolling together as to be
Flowing graceful shimmering sea
Into the field of life

The first step is hard to take
The second may even break
The beating pattern of my heart
Raising, falling swaying apart
Tender pedals falling to the ground
Circling in the air all around
Into the field of life

Sunshine caress by body
Touch my limb, my heart, my soul
Wrap your sweet rays into me
As if to say and to know
My thoughts on this crooked path
Seeking joyful peace not wrath

Into this field of life

The Confident Man

Look deep, enter, and see
What is it troubling me?

Could it be fear of being harmed?
Burning into the soul's alarm

Searching for the one *Confident Man*
Taking a risk in giving both hands
A chance of reality into this life
Now possibly of being a good wife

Finding a *Confident Partner* in which to play
Full wind into sails each mysterious day
Removing the history of pain and sorrow
Far away to yesterday not in tomorrow

Playing with me and taking the part

A Man with Confidence of the heart
Confident is the *Man,* his knowledge of the plan
The future in us to believe, for hope in man

With The Confident Man

The Race Continued On

The man came from nowhere
As I gazed across the dock
Our lips smiled and our eyes locked
Hearts racing together

And the race continued on
Sailboats passing in the wind
Tacking with each gust to send
One further than the other
Nor did us would it bother

And the interview began
The hope, the dream as the same
Fulfilling what seemed to be
Placing in the wrongful blame
Only hidden liquid secrets in thee

And the signals of Danger ahead
With the full sails flying
No marker in your sight
Taking the vessel not blowing
In irons in the flight

And all is lost and gone
So fix your sails another way
Find happiness and play
Turn the wheel to the sun
No longer shall you run

And the Race Continued On

Forever In Time

Crushing waves to shore
As the moon hides behind the cloud
With the wind sounding roar
Hearing a voice faintly so loud

Can you catch the wind?
Can you catch the moonbeams?
Can you see waves blend?
Can you see what I have seen?

Sending shivers to my soul
Taking each inch of my body
A touch that is much like a hold
Speaking softly somewhere in me

Can you catch the wind?
Can you catch the moonbeams?
Can you see the waves blend?
Can you see what I have seen?

Looking through the dead tree
As the moon surrounding rays
This was done before with thee
Saying long ago from today

(continued)

Can you catch the wind?
Can you catch the moonbeams?
Can you see the waves blend?
Can you see what I redeem?

Reflecting on the time before
Fluttering of my delicate heart
Leaving me desiring much more
Recalling not wanting for us to part

Can you catch the wind?
Can you catch the moonbeams?
Can you see the waves blend?

Can you capture this scene?

Forever In Time

Yesterday, Today, and Tomorrow

Yesterday

A chance, a meeting
Somewhere retreating
Into life without a plan
But time sifting through sand

A smile, a boyish look
Grasping pleasure took
Repeating a childhood sameness
Different places no less

Similarities are there
As clear as the morning, air
To breathe a new delight
Friendship, newness polite

A hand reached out to say
Come with me and let's play
From coast to coast
To life we toast

(continued)

Today

My heart my soul take a peak
Through laughter I seek
A peace from within
At last without sin

I am what you see
Not trouble free
But a smile to speak
Sensuous week

Tomorrow

I cannot speak for tomorrow
Only stolen time to borrow
From this tenuous self-built wall
For tomorrow's are in yesterdays
And yesterdays are kept in today

Remembering your glance
And charming romance
On cliffs by the Pacific Ocean
A kiss, a touch feeling the motion

From crashing waves far below
Happiness to you bestow

Yesterday, Today, and Tomorrow

Missing You

In every way

Missing you
How do I say
That I love you
Trust and want you

Missing you
I say a prayer

Missing you
That you know I care
How do I ever let you know?
I'm with you wherever you go

Missing you
Makes time to stand still

Missing you
Makes my day dreams real
In each moment that pass

Keeping feelings that last

Missing you

The Touch

The sensation of the touch
The touch - making me come alive
Electrical impulses rush
Throbbing within my thighs

Gently over my body
Blinding to my senses

The Touch, the sensations
Awakening the desire
Leaving no contemplation
How can this go higher?

Gently over my body
Blinding to my senses

The touch, the hand
Crossing ecstasy with pleasure
Only oneness who can
Find a way to measure

Gently over my body
Blinding to my senses

The hands that touch
Breathlessly I say
The touch is so much
With you I lay

Gently over my body
Blinding to my senses

The Touch

My Valentine

*D*esire, the feeling in my soul
*E*lation taking a strong role
*N*urture the new love in my heart
*N*ow us together not to part
*I*solating each minute counted in time
*S*pending eternity with my Valentine

*M*aking my soul rise up and see
*O*ffering thy love tenderly
*R*aising our hands to meet
*R*apture in your touch of me
*I*ncreasing the rhythm of love
*S*eeking the peace from above
*O*nly to find tranquility
*N*earness of the intimacy

With My Valentine

Two Souls

Three times two souls do meet
Exchange a glance, a smile, a look
Three times by chance to greet
Two strangers from beyond it took

To capture that special feeling
Sharing stories the whole night
The past-history rekindling
The sorrow, the dream, the plight

Three times two souls do meet
Exchanging glances, a look, a smile
Three times by chance, eyes see
With you in closeness to reconcile

What happened in the years?
So near but yet far away
Through happiness and tears
Working hard no time to play

Three times two souls do meet
Exchange a glance, a smile, a look
Same acquaintances seek
Like the last chapter in a book

To today sharing stories old
The intimacy not known
With other lovers never told
But together to be shown

(continued)

Three times two souls do meet
Exchanging glances, a look, a smile
Never in life repeats
To be Cinderella for a while

With Two Souls

The Mystery

The mystery, the look
Glances to each other
Sensation took
Finding a lover

Not seeking one another
Knowing through the years
Why should we bother?
With all our fears

The mystery, the look
Glances to each other
A smile that made us shook
Can you see? Have you heard?

Afraid of what will be
Holding me in your arms
What is the sacred key?
To save us from all harm

The mystery, the look
Glances to each other
The sound of the bubbling brook
Time passing as if water

Take my hand let the wind blow
Heading for pleasures not known
Wherever we may go
Never shall the two be alone

(continued)

The mystery, the look
Glances to each other
Taking only what is took
Changing life to smoother

Take one day at a time
See what tomorrow brings
Wanting you to be mine
Softly the angels sing

The mystery, the look
Glances to each other
Life is an open book
Reading the first chapter

Of the Mystery

Holding Me

Hold me in your arms
Away from all harms
Dream of sailing away
Breathlessly for the day

A chance meeting
Love not seeking
Just to open the door
In walked you, no more

Hold me in your arms
With your simple charms
Never would I dream
Life could be serene

A chance meeting
A smile greeting
Reaching your hands
With no demands

Hold me in your arms
Feeling close, so warm
Taking me as no other
Never to be another

Holding me

Kiss my Soul

I'm so afraid
Of tomorrow
My life is frayed
Sad with sorrow

Kiss my lips
Reach my soul
Seek my heart
Watching I told

I'm so afraid
My life protect
Just you have made
Love resurrect

Kiss my hand
Touch my soul
Take my heart
Keep me whole

I'm so afraid
Of distant past
As I will lay
In your love, surpass

Kiss my breast
Speak not to me
Now I rest
Always with thee

Not afraid

Love

Are you the love of my life?
Are you the one?
My dream, your dream, within all dreams
The once spoken words for this scene

I open my life to you
Redrawing the colors for us to see
Searching inside us for two
Playing, kissing in rapture of me

Are you the love of my life?
Did I meet you before?
Were you the one I hear calling?
Or was it my own voice speaking

Open thy strong arms
I softly feel your masculine part
Spoken are the charms
Revitalize the damaged heart

Are you the love of my life?
Will you always stay?
Will time be the lasting one?
Or the truth played until done

"Hello Love of My Life"

Secrets

The Secrets not old
Sacred not to be told
Come to me tonight
Making life a delight

Take me into your life
Cutting fears as a knife
Catch me oh so gently
Opening eyes blindly

I want to be a part
Of everything you are
Waking up in the morning
Seeking the slightest warning

Take me into your arms
Keeping me from any harm
Melt away the fears
Shutting out the tears

Tell me how I make you feel
I want to know if you are real
The smile on your face
Happiness to trace

Take me on an adventure
Discovering simple pleasures
Tasting rain upon our bodies
Salty, moist, wet drops embodied

(continued)

In silent Secrets not told
To me but left in your soul
My love, come to me tonight
Making our life appear right

Secrets Taking Me

Valentine

Joy fulfilled our lives
On the evening that we met
Now to be husband and wife
So happy we are no regrets
In love with you my Valentine
Eager to start our future plan
With the one holding us divine
Etched infinitely in the sand
Reaching for us tenderly from above
Sailing together, forever my love
**Through the Endless Time
Be My Valentine**

Going Away

River of Friends

Bearing their souls, their hearts at the splendid ravine

Going from Hueco Falls and ending on the Gruene

Sharing their deep secrets along the way

Making each one feel special for the day

Telling their stories for all to believe

Showing kindness in each history

Accepting both sharp and smooth parts

Keeping one safe from treacherous hearts

Pulling you through the currents at last

Bridging today with the recent past

Gliding in the coolness, the glimmering

Seeing beauty and remembering

Escaping from the heat in the maze

Playing with the new soul mates, they stop and gaze

Surrounding angels gently floating around

Leaving with peace at River Road Camp Grounds

Trusting the tradition shall never end

Staying forever with your River of Friends

The Eclipse

The dawn came

The home run

All not same

Heads were hung

In despair

No wind

God to care

Floating

Rain danced

As never before

Wind pranced

In sheer down pour

Out in a distance

A ship appeared

God sent 'The Eclipse'

La Dulce Vida cheered

A wonderful plan

(continued)

That people exist

Good Samaritans

To friends assist

In a long, harden journey

Towing each step of the way

Always be grateful to thee

Thanking God and you each day

Howling at the Moon

Four sailors went a sailing
Werewolf cruise to Heald Bank moonlight held
Dolphins were a playing
Three on port – three on starboard all identical

Alongside two turtles came
Wahoo lost seen by one
King fish caught mackerel same
Quickly time passed down the sun

Stopping the boat to swim
A rope overboard not to lose
The crew from currents grim
Enjoying the salty Gulf so blue

The trusty sailors sailed the far side of West Heald Bank
Thirty miles to 207A rig
No one mutinies or walked the jagged plank
But all did a brawny drunken jig

The boat rocked back and forth to and fro
No fish were caught in hand
The crew from currents grim
Sickness left heave ho

The master baiter kept three fish and let go eight
The tolerance limit left for all the fishes
Only the turtle challenged the rate
Trying to save the endangered species

(continued)

At last the trip ended
Lost from our sight Wind River
Only La Dulce Vida ascended
Home safely a believer

Howling at the Moon

Crawfish Festival

Have you ever been to the Crawfish Festival?

The on down in the bayou of Breaux Bridge, Louisiana
Cajun cooking that will spice your life and taste buds delectable
And make you sing as no coon ass can sing soprano
Dance until your feet won't move anymore
And make you play until your eyes explore
The other Crawfish festival not Cajun but Creole
With the rhythms, that engulfs your soul
Cajun? Creole? Which one is the best?
Either place you will surely be blessed!

At the Crawfish Festival

Kerrville Folk Festival

Just look around what do you see?
A reflection of silent yesterdays
Of flower children happily
Singing tunes of peace marching this way
Hair braided with beads flowing through
Tie-dye shirts, skirts, dresses adieu
A serenity surrounding these children
Seeking safety in this dusty glen
Singing phrases of a time long ago
Some capturing happiness some not so

Just look around and what do you see?
A reflection of yester years to believe
The folk Festival you can escape
And be what once was thought a mistake
It is a music world, with words that surround the sounds
At each part gently caressing you up and down
Breathing the long ago old essence of life
Until all the music has gone and broken in strife
Back to the world that cannot stay
To all that is kept sacred in yesterday

In Kerrville

The Beach

Feet moving the warm hot sand
Between the toes to the land
Waves rushing forward to meet
Your body tender it will greet

Blue swells touching every piece
Foam rinsing all parts beneath
Of secrets kept for centuries
The pattern searching in series

Of up and down to and fro
Certainly as if to know
Not only secrets from the past
But the future happiness at last

At the Beach – Myrtle Beach

Waves

Sparkling, glimmering sea
Rise up coming toward thee

Warmth between the toes
Seeking the shapes, it knows
Of mystery tales from the past
Hidden far below at last

Watch the foam
As it roams
Tiny the bubbles making one
Connecting under the sun

Never leaving what once was blue
Never seeing what now was true
But the perpetual motion
Satisfying to the notion

Sparkling glimmering sea
Rise up coming toward thee

Waves
Myrtle Beach, SC

Time

Time passes
A glance
Happiness
Romance

Tomorrow
Say Good-bye
Bring Sorrow
As I fly

Away for now
But not forever
Tell me how
To be so clever

The White Mountains – Laughing
Echo Lake – canoeing
The Sunset Lodge – Dining
Cozy Cottage – Loving

Seeing yesterday
In your eyes
Your world today
Each surprise

Thanking you
You are so kind
Sight seen true
Until next Time

Tijuana

Children with eyes so wide
Coming up to your side
With their hands out begging
In sorrow neglecting

As you turn away
You can go and play
With music and dance
And feeling of romance

Or you can go and buy
Barter not to be so high
Leather, jewelry plentiful
Keeping the price within the duel

The last the Margarita flow
Pouring into your body to sow
The party life throughout the night
In darkness seeking the fun light

Bodies that once was selling
Now their bodies propelling
Come enjoy my charms
I will keep you from harm

Magical is Tijuana, Mexico
Until the dawn I must go
Across the border into USA
Good-bye for now, adios, I must say

Tijuana

Clear Blue Water

Deep in the clear blue water
Gliding just knowing the way
The sails and lines hard over
To venture in seas we play

From West Palm Beach to West End
Buying conch and lobster to sweet
Anchoring just in the sand
Boat slipping away while asleep

Deep in the clear blue water
Gliding just knowing the way
Salvaging a basket part
To take from yesterday

From West End to Great Sale
Dinghy to coral shore
Using the engine not the sail
Nothing there to explore

Deep in the clear blue water
Gliding just knowing the way
The sails and lines maneuver
To venture in seas we say

From Great Sale to Carter Cay
Exploring the sore of conch shells
Bahamians singingly
Not waiting but taking quick sail

(continued)

Deep in the clear blue water
Gliding just knowing the way
Turtles and fishing as dover
To peril in seas they play

From Carter Cay to the Fox Town
Having dinner at Shell Café
Playing and drinking Kalik down
High seas in dinghy to May Day

Deep in the clear blue water
Gliding just knowing the way
Dolphins playing together
In the bow parting to play

From Fox Town in Spanish Cay
The rich and famous hide
Seeking all the privacy
Hide away from their demise

Snorkeling and fighting the current
Beautiful sunset at dinner
The touch, the kiss, the living spent
The peace in the days forever

Deep in the clear blue water
Gliding just knowing the way
The sails and lines hard over
To venture in seas we play

(continued)

Making the way back to Great Sale
Stopping at Mangrove Cay
A quick dip from the rail

Speedy return to West Palm Beach

Deep in the clear blue water
Gliding just knowing the way
Seeking home with sails hard over
The venture ending the play

In the Clear Blue Water
Abacos, Bahamas

Wispy Clouds

The wispy clouds up above
The wind softly upon thy face
Kisses returned making love
Hearts together the challenging race

Watching the sunrise early in the morn
Playing on the waves to shore
Gentleness with each other born
Seeking ourselves to be explored

Selecting shells along the way
Feet prints left in the sand
Taking time for children's play
Kissing the salt from thy hand

Feeling thy body the warmth the sun
Lying with you side by side
Resting, laughing just for fun
By the blue liquid so wide

Swelling waves to earth
The perfect timing of the dive
It must be sensing the match
Falling backward and forward in the stride

Eating Cuban food delight
Romance, music in the air
Listening to jazz late one night
Only having the simplest of cares

(continued)

The wispy clouds up above
The wind softly upon thy face
Kisses in twined making love
Sadly leaving the mystical place

Cocoa Beach, Florida

Sensuous Poems Through Time *by Renne'*

Hidden Away

High in the North Carolina mountains area
Just hidden away from all to see
A retreat in Murphy for only two to share
Exploring each other secretly

Each day with newness is recovered
Your body to rapture mine
Kisses so gently discovered
Smiles, happiness so blind

Having breakfast lunch and dinner
Watching TV and movies in bed
Laughing between him and her
Noticing just us not what was said

Finding my special treasures and keepsakes
At Fosters the local Flea Market rest
Eating at Tuckers southern buffet
Peanut butter chocolate pie the best

Snow began to fall on Wednesday morn
Bringing us smiles and such delight
In the surrounding freshness born
Throwing snowballs in playful fight

(continued)

Walking down the steep ravine
To McDonalds farm nestled below
The beauty, the forest, the scene
Keeping each other warm with our glow

High in the North Carolina Mountain air
Hidden away from all to see
Just remembering the touch, we share
Captured always in my heart with thee

Hidden Away

Caribbean Music

Sensuous notes on thy body
Sounds of the torrid romance
Seek thy own soul totally free
Lost to the beat in a trance

Hearing music of the Caribbean
Dancing revived from years ago
Sway to the tropical rhythm
Make all wrong into right so

Passing ages through the years
Fading youth into tears
No longer should thy care
Left are all the fears

Touching the distance gone
Wishing the child to return
A kiss, a dance, a song
The love always will it burn

Listening to mysterious tones
Capturing the one heart
Sail away into the night wind blown
The future will us part

Sensuous notes on my body
Sounds of the torrid romance
Seek my own soul totally free
Lost with the beat in the trance

Music in the Caribbean

Take Me Caribbean

The secrets of the islands
Not known to any man
Are hidden underneath
Protected the sacred reef

Take me into your arms
Pleasure me with your charms
Flowing softly to each part
Stealing away the fleshy heart

So tender is the coral
The tiny fish into a wall
A sea horse washed ashore
Back to the sea ever more

Take us into your arms
Pleasure us with your charms
Seeking safety in the play
Morning, noon, and all the day

Turtles swim by so fast
Five barracuda pass
Sea urchins not to touch
Busy the sea life as such

Take you into my arms
Pleasure thee with my charms
Kissing in the sun rays
Holding each other all day

Starfish hide in the sand
Sea Rays stay far from land
Sea fans softly swaying
To and fro as playing

(continued)

Take thee into your arms
Pleasure me by thy charms
Engulfing moonbeam rays
Glowing endlessly today

Take me Caribbean

Seeking

The Icy Palace
Covered in snow
Delicate Lace
Comfort and glow

Flashing fast downhill
Laughing to the thrill
Lovers holding hands
Crossing frosty land

The Icy palace
In the Rockies high
Away from the race
Reaching to the sky

Driving through hidden pathways
Giggling with happiness and play
The danger not aware
No sign of any scare

The Icy Palace
The white wonderland
A secret place
With closeness at hand

Always Seeking
Vail, Colorado

Paradise

*The Island sun
Calls to us all
Hearing the fun
Waiting the fall*

Wakening the soul
Touching your body
Rising just to see
Wanting not to be told

*By the Island sun
Calling to us all
Breathing life to one
Not catching the fall*

The wind in my hair
Blowing in your face
My body so bare
Not leaving a trace

*In the Island sun
Calling to us all
Shaping of a run
Breaking the fall*

Kissing your sweet moist lips
Tasting the mixture of us
Chills in your finger tips
Breathlessly the lovers rush

(continued)

*From the Island sun
Called to us all
Leaving not to be done
Ending of the fall*

In Paradise
Nassau Bahamas

Belize

The beauty of the water
The silence of the wind
Making sounds of laughter
With us starting to begin

Our anniversary of only one year
Taking us to new heights
Snorkeling without fear
Through reefs beauty delights

Seeing coral colors indescribable
Marine life for eyes unknown
Moray eels, spotted stingrays, and sea turtles
God created all alone

Taking trips deep into the jungle low
Seeing Mayan ruins kept secret
Another time so long ago
Buried into temples not to weep

San Pedro the friendly place
Away from all the craziness
Simpler life; much slower pace
Where you can certainly take rest

In Belize

The Ride

The chill of the sea
Is calling to me
Catch the wave
Let me save

In the crystal blue
Cold beyond you knew
Seeking the right time
Only in rhyme

Crushing upon thee
Barely do you see
The water above
Certain that you love

In the confused surf
It is my own turf
Waiting wake for me to pick
The Ride in the Pacific

With the Ride

Huntington Beach, California

Harvest Moon Delight

Adventure on the open seas
For Harvest Moon 2003
The CAT had luxury
The crew safely will be

In winds clocked 360 degrees
Southeast south and ending in the east
Sometimes ferocious as a wild beast
Then as gently like a soft lamb's breeze

Adventure on the open seas
For the Harvest Moon 2003
The captain and crew sailed through the night
Much to the passengers delight

Rain Storms brought much needed winds
20 to 25 knots left a grin
Ride 'em cowboy in the saddle again
Steadily pushing through waves at hand

Adventure on the Open Seas
For Harvest Moon 2003
The wind died in the middle of the night
Sadly, engines began ending the flight

Port Aransas making their way
To find the marina party and play
For us to meet the challenge and say
Another year another day

Harvest Moon In Sight

(continued)

The Return

Eventful return from Harvest Moon
Left injured crewmember to soon

Going down the ICW
Sunken marker broken rudder

Taking on water be alert
Captain Bill quickly makeshift part

Reality Check is now at home
Pier 77 in Galveston

Waiting the damaged rudder to be whole
Safely back to Marina del Sol

Next Year for Harvest Moon Delight

Chihuahua

Poor El Ranchero hidden in the desert
Away from all to see
Only family plays and meet together
Sharing café and tea

Sound of the laughter
Music surrounding
Playful touching gestures
Happiness gleam

Riding horses to Buffalo
All eyes watching
From windows high and low
Whispers of gringos talking

Sounds of the laughter
Music surrounding
Playful touching gestures
Happiness gleam

Jimenez go for dancing
Carlos owner of Bar Bronco
Eduardo strums guitar and sings
Anita proud of peacock so

Sounds of the laughter
Music surrounding
Playful touching gesture
Happiness gleam

(continued)

Last day still "No comprende"
Trying to talk in Spanish
How do I say Familia Grande
To you such wealth I wish

Sounds of laughter
Music surrounding
Playful touching gesture
Happiness gleam

In Chihuahua

Sensuous Poems Through Time *by Renne'*

Life Disarray

Looking Out the Window

I sit and look out the misty window
No one on the other side
No laughing, no hiding from the sorrow
Nowhere, no way can I hide

From the emptiness I feel
Thinking I would somehow heal
Broken promises, broken truths
Only the fragile soul bruised

Why should I be here again?
Wanting happiness not sin
Risking my safe world, I created
From all misery I so hated

Turning from one love to another
Hoping that each would not be the other
But patterns never die
Atlas the same old lie

I sit and look out the stormy window
No one on the other side
No laughing, no hiding from my sorrow
Nowhere, no way can I hide

From the Window

Naked

Naked is the soul
Using the last breath
Heartless lust that told
In heaviness wanting to rest

Make my day
Come and lay
Not thinking of all the timeless sins
Never to be relentless again

Naked is the soul
Who knows no end?
But champion the fold
Missing colors within

Black today
White I pray
Seeking compromise

Please do not demise

Naked is the soul
Cover thyself with warmth
And wrap your arms to hold
Gently as not to burn

Naked is the soul
When no one will ever hear
The bells that toll

Ringing softly in your ear

(continued)

So naked ever to be
Until you will see
Naked is your soul
For all eternity

Is your soul

The Fear

A woman sits alone

No one seeing

No one hearing

Gray hair falling down

Hands crooked around

No one cares

No one dares

Eating without grace

Features without a face

Lifeless of heart

Happiness apart

Calling to one

Wanting to run

But the Fear

Keeps the tears

Streaming through day-to-day

Gleaming to silent prey

To no one but

The Fear

A Little Girl

Once upon a time a little girl came
Deep within the inner self
Feelings of personal blame

No self-esteem left

One morning the sun rose
And the rain brought tears
Feelings from toes to nose
Raining inward, outward fears

A hand was held to keep touch
Each finger sensitive
Wanting happiness so much
Peace tranquil, but pensive

The little girl laughed with each new tear
Bringing the child to a new dimension
Finding the peace and happiness without the fear
At last realizing the omission

Once upon a time a little girl came
Wishing for happiness ever more
Finding herself whole and sane

Starting the new journey to explore

The Little Girl Found

Say Good-bye to Silence

No sound I hear
Not even a whisper
Just echoes of silence
And broken promises

Say good-bye to what use to be
Or ever could have been
Never, no never to sin
Please forgive me God so holy

I tried one more time
To break the pattern
To make him only mine
The light gone dark the lantern

Reaching for renewed happiness lost
Tossing respect and feeling away
Self-esteem suffering it cost
To find the answer I pray

Now I can go to seek myself
And always will I love thy self
Forever in thee belong
Silence broken into song

Good-bye to Silence

My Son

Why are you angry son?

Have I not been what I could?
Putting you forward and beyond
What else could I do?

You are so important to me
Such brightness and quick a smile
So close, you are to me
And growing up all the while

Why are you angry son?
You have all you should.
To us you do no wrong
What else could I do?

Let me see you grow
To realize and know
The importance of family
And all the familiarity

Why are you angry son?
You have ones that would
Making your life so wrong
What else could I do?

(continued)

Try to see the happiness of home
Be together and belong
With mother, sister, father and grandmother
Standing beside you before no other

Why are you angry son?

Take Me Wind

I touched happiness
And felt the wind across my face
It turned to confusion
And took my breath away

The wind blows and blows
Coming from all directions
Lifting my hair in disarray
Playing, teasing with my soul

Sometimes it's abrupt
Like the blackness of dark
Losing the way down corridors
And walking in the unknown of blindness

Tell me wind which way do you go
Please lift me up into oneness
Make the feeling into happiness
Forever the coolness the comfort of your arms

Take Me Wind

Shadows

Shadows block the face
Hidden in black widow's lace
Transferring thoughts to lies
Brilliant in the disguise

Sheltered in loving arms
Transferring death and harm
Silk the skin is to touch
Hypnotize the breath to rush

Like a kaleidoscope of many colors
Changing from within quickening each blur
Hand to heart, laughter to tears
Silence to silence quiets the fears

Engulfed in sorrow
Pain tomorrow
Shadows the face
Hidden no trace

Only Shadows

Change O' Heart

Seeking a new way of life
Not knowing what is to come
But learning what was *before*

The untold calmness
I shouted within my soul
Speaking of peace no changes, I *implore*

Feeling the body
Floating across the bay into the sea
Gracefully entering the *door*

Touching the Wind

Of lightness bringing in sails
Waves with a *roar*

Through the sun, the day, the night
Hearing in the wind 'Change O' Heart'
As a bird I do *soar*

Rejoice

As the darkness falls
Turn thy head to see the light
Think of times to recall
The continuous journey, the flight

Help me God take the pain
Into life I do remain
Seeking no one to take blame
Before you, I am lame

This has been my home
Solitude all along
I am not to belong
Take me your throne

Hold me close in your arms
Comfort me with your charms
Keep me away from life's harm
In eternity, keep me warm

Rejoicing as the darkness falls
Turning thy head to see the light
Thinking of times to recall
The ending, the journey, the flight

Rejoice

The Sadness

Take away the heavy sadness
Wipe the tears from your eyes
Erase those hideous lies
Find hope, love sanctity, and rest

What was done in yesterday
Can no longer be today
Plan for your tomorrow
Take away the sorrow

Hide away quickly to your haven
Hear the water shore sounds
Listen to tones around
Happiness nearing the next bend

What was done in yesterday
Can no longer be today
Plan for your tomorrow
Take away the sorrow

Your child continues to grow
Always in your heart
Will stay safely a part
And will find a way to know

What was done in yesterday
Can no longer be today
Plan for your tomorrow
Take away the sorrow

Forget the past silence
Return your voice
Seek to rejoice
With no more repentance

(continued)

What was done in yesterday
Can no longer be today
Plan for your tomorrow

Take away the sorrow

The Sadness

Wispy Clouds

The wispy clouds up above
The wind so softly upon thy face
Kisses returned, making love
Hearts together the challenging race

Watching the sunrise early in the morn
Playing on the rolling waves to shore
Being so gentle with each other born
Seeking our selves to be explored

Selecting shells along the way
Leaving foot prints in the sand
Taking the time for children's play
Kissing the salt from thy hand

Feeling thy body, the warmth, the sun
Laying together, side by side
Resting, caring, laughing just for fun
Nearing the blue liquid so wide

Swelling waves to the shore
Timing of the perfect dive
Sensing it must be more
Falling forward in the stride

Eating Cuban food of such a delight
Romancing music in the warm air
Listening to jazz late one night
Having only the simplest of cares

(continued)

The wispy clouds up above
The wind so softly upon thy face
Kisses entwined, making love
Sadly leaving this mystical place

Cocoa Beach, Florida

Messages

No thoughts are left unsaid
Interpretations from the head
Lost Messages in time
Only Hope in mind

What was said not heard
Listening to every word
New Message in time
Only hope in mind

No ringing, do I hear
Are you OK? I fear
Old message in time
Only hope in mind

So I keep your messages
Repeating the passages
Just one at a time
Looking for a sign

In Your Messages

A Silent Kiss

A silent kiss
On your sweet lips
Something amiss
The endless rip

Between two lovers
Wanting different goals
Seeing each other
Not sharing their souls

A silent kiss
On your forehead
Seeing the sunrise
No longer said

Only one speaking
With an open heart
Not in the meeting
Forcing tears apart

A silent kiss
On your smooth cheek
No more bliss
In you I seek

Walking away
Down another path
Only to say
Too late in aftermath

(continued)

*A silent kiss
Onto your hair
Taking the risk
No longer there*

Gone but the memories
Of only the touches the kiss
One of life's stories
Of lost love to always miss

*A silent kiss
On your soft hand
Awakening this
Silence again*

Words

How can I put this into words and say?
The reckless wind blew me from you away
So head strong into foul weather
Leaving me without a tether
Drifting aimlessly all alone
The heart empty feeling wrong

How can I put this into words and say?
That I made a mistake and lost my way
Now trying to find my way home
Into your arms where I belong
Make the tenderness into your heart
A safe place for us to never part

How can I put this into words and say?
Can you find forgiveness today?
Let us begin our journey again
I as your woman and you as my man
Our Souls and Spirits intertwined
Taking my hand one day at a time

How can I put this into words and say?
The only words left "I love you today"

Words

Silence

The silence breaks apart
A little each day
Expectations Play
Separating the heart

Where have you gone?
Where do you go?
Leaving me alone
In darkness woe

In night to wonder
Naked in my flesh
Reading in the stars
Myself only to caress

Where have you gone?
Where do you go?
Leaving me alone
In darkness low

Wrapping my arms around
Feeling the smoothness
The soft skin tight and abound
Seeking sleep and rest

Where have you gone?
Where do you go?
Leaving me alone
In darkness, grow

Speak to me from afar
Let me hear your call
Break the silence apart
Sharing me with all

(continued)

Where have you gone?
Where do you go?
Leaving me alone
In darkness, know

With Silence

Stand Still My Husband

Sunshine comes to the one who believes in God, in himself
Inner goodness comes within to the one who waits
Sacrifice is difficult, not always fair until left
Payment is judged by those who commiserate
Stand still absorb the light and seek your soul
The man, the challenge, the immediate goal

Stand Still My Husband

I Love You

It will come

The Mask

Take off the mask
Show me who you are
Don't make me ask
In truth to explore

Walk with me this day
Let us seek and play
In the warmth the sun
Make our life just fun

Hidden in the mask
Show me who you are
Speak the truth at last
Empty ever more

The warmth of your body
Blinding me to the real thee
The softness of your kiss
Touches lightly into bliss

Take off the mask
Show me who you are
Silence of your past
Secrets from the shore

Don't tell me your lies
Behind this disguise
In where our destiny goes
Child like giving as one knows

(continued)

*Off is the mask
I know not who you are
Broken the trust
Empty hopes do soar*

The Masks

Can You Hear?

The cries of the children
Heard across the land
Falling high from their sins
Holding with no hands

Why has this happened?
Tell me, whom do we blame?
Someone must be mistaken
Truly, they were insane

Pictures imprinted in our minds
Forever will they not be erased?
Looking for a reasonable sign
Taking precious life into death chased

The cries of the children
Heard across the land
Calling out to all men
Each to unite and band

Why has this happened?
Tell me whom do we blame
Together our brothers united
This life gone into flames

Hearing the cries
Twin Towers - 09/11/01

Sensuous Poems Through Time *by Renne'*

Life

Years go by
No one notices
Youth will die
Letting us miss

The Days
The words
The play
To serve

Seek the young
Take us away
Not to run
Seizing the Play

A Kiss
Of leisure
The Bliss
To Measure

Take the Time
Feel the Youth
See the Sign
Know the truth

Each second
The presence
The moment
Remembrance

To Live

PASSING TO STAY

Large Foreheads

Have you ever seen a Rocket Scientist?
Strange words flow from this linguist
Using the square root and major modes
To determine the navigational loads

What is the common delineation?
Large Foreheads used for contemplation
Wide Space between hairline and brow
Explain their smart mind somehow

But yet one must remember gorillas have large foreheads too
Could this be the missing link? Could it be true?
Yes, it must be what one would logically suspect
So I will continue to research and inspect

Large Foreheads (Onboard Shuttle)

Sensuous Poems Through Time *by Renne'*

Thirty Years

Thirty years have passed
Since we shared our space
Clothes decorated in dainty lace
Our room a total mess

Your presence was always held
A goddess, a mentor to me
Surrounded by all who felt
Your beauty and kindness to see

Now in the middle of our years
Seeing you fight so hard
Health complexities I fear
Seeking answers near and far

With problems, you are a rock
Doing always right
Feeling the total pain lock
Guiding soul to purest light

Sharing yourself again with me
Thirty years has been too long
Giving dreams unselfishly
Now united, we belong

Thirty More Years

Delicate Rose

You are so very small
Then before I know it

Change comes

Small buds, vibrant colors
Large petals, sweet scents

Change comes

Embracing, surrounding
With the beauty of life

Delicate Rose

Flying High

Flying high above the clouds
Seeking solace from the shrouds

Multi-color each piece in hidden
From all that is forbidden

As if to shout from within
Stop and see the different shapes
Each one an individual blend
Playing hide and seek to form a face

A face that has no eyes
Nor a heart or should I surmise
But shadows perfectly placed
With softness of woven lace

Look at the face and see below
The body of land flourishes so
Pieces and parts like a puzzle fit
Making a game to follow I submit

High above the clouds you can hear
Laughter permeated with a cheer
Gently floating within you dear
God's happiness seeking no fear

But peace surrounding the clouds so high
Floating the darkness away the lie
No tears, no pain, no harm I pray
Flying high safely in the array

The Artist Within

Surrounding colors come alive
Blending techniques and styles
Capturing realness with dreams
Finding sensual passion serene

Take a look and what do you see
But a Latin man who hides
Behind the colors that bleed
Beyond his years to abide

Just a man with brush in hand
Choosing subjects from the mind
From portraits to faraway lands
Creating forms from the blind

Shaping the soul with each stroke
Not knowing where the reflection may go
Once asleep inside now awoke
Into a journey of an artist's woe

Each medium has a life of its own
Speaking among the lost images
No longer a silent space not known
But lasting renditions though all ages

Surrounding colors come alive
Blending techniques and styles
Capturing realness with dreams
Finding sensual passion serene

Within An Artist

Images

Softly delicately through ages
Seeing myself again in images

Hiding from life and death
Only younger underneath
The years away chased

The days, the months turn to years
Falling rain covered in my tears

Softly delicately through ages
Seeing myself again in images

Making life childlike play
Finding secret passages
The years away chased
One door opening the next
Channeling through the text

Softly delicately through ages
Seeing myself again in images

Separating the heart

The Collector

Come and all you gather
Midst of the precious art
Each piece is a story
Wanting all the glory

The search, an adventure
Into life did seek
Through different cultures
The bearded one did peek

Come and you gather
Midst of priceless art
Surround yourself briefly
Crafts made so tenderly

Each hung with such precision
Throughout the museum room
Providing the illusion
Of empty souls in bloom

Come and I gather
Midst of sacred art
Touching each special piece
Throughout eternity

With the Collector

Guiding Light

You are my guiding Light
Always close by my side
Showing me what was right
During Life's bumpy ride

You gave me precious life
That day long ago
Tenderness of a wife
With loving me so

You never judged me
During my times of trouble
Always sympathy
With kind sweet thoughts so noble

You are my guiding Light
My love continues to grow
Never will I lose sight
My Mother I Love You so

My Guiding Light

Check other books published by Renne' Siewers:

The Last Payload: The MECS Experiment
Publish America
The Kings Payload: The MECS Experiment
www.createspace.com/3729974
-
Nighty Night Sailboat Children's books:
Nighty Night Sailboat (sailing terms)
www.createspace.com/3729974
Nighty Night Sailboat Goes to Spain (Spanish culture)
www.createspace.com/3823482
Santa finds Nighty Night Sailboat (children who move or may not be home for Christmas)
www.createspace.com/3833136

Soon to come:
Nighty Night Sailboat in the Bahamas (Bahamian culture
www.createspace.com/3919360
Nighty Night Sailboat Adventures in Italy (Italian culture)
Nighty Night Sailboat Celebrates Key West Birthday (What to do in Key West)
Nighty Night Sailboat takes Juni to the Hospital (going to the hospital)
Nighty Night Sailboat visits Mount Vernon (Home of our first President)

Check out Amazon
or
www.sailadybooks.blogspot.com

Sensuous Poems Through Time *by Renne'*

Renne' and her husband Jon travel on their sailboat from port-to-port.

Made in the USA
Middletown, DE
01 February 2019